Can I Tell You About...

Compassion?

A Guide for Friends, Family and Professionals

Sue Webb

Illustrated by Rosy Salaman

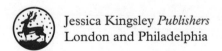
Jessica Kingsley *Publishers*
London and Philadelphia

First published in 2018
by Jessica Kingsley Publishers
73 Collier Street
London N1 9BE, UK
and
400 Market Street, Suite 400
Philadelphia, PA 19106, USA

www.jkp.com

Library of Congress Cataloging in Publication Data
A CIP catalog record for this book is available
from the Library of Congress

British Library Cataloguing in Publication Data
A CIP catalogue record for this book is
available from the British Library

ISBN 978 1 78592 466 8
eISBN 978 1 78450 848 7

Printed and bound in Great Britain

Learning Resource Centre
Park Road, Uxbridge, Middlesex, UB8 1NQ
Renewals: 01895 853344

Please return this item to the LRC on or before the
last date stamped below:

STORYTELLING

CAN I TELL YOU ABOUT...?

The 'Can I tell you about...?' series offers simple introductions to a range of conditions, issues and big ideas that affect our lives. Friendly characters invite readers to learn about their experiences, share their knowledge, and teach us to empathise with others. These books serve as excellent starting points for family and classroom discussions.

Other subjects covered in the Can I tell you about...? series

CONTENTS

INTRODUCTION: CHARACTER AND VALUES

Everybody has *character* traits.

When people talk about having a good character, they are describing the traits of a person's personality that make them think and act in a good way. It's about how they form and build relationships with other people, how they treat living things and also how they treat themselves.

Just about all people can show positive and negative, or good and bad, character traits. In this book, we are going to focus on the positive side of people. Good character traits include aspects such as being kind, honest, responsible and respectful. These character traits are also called 'values'.

Everybody has positive *values* that are important to them. When you see someone making a 'good choice', they could be using positive values such as respect, honesty, kindness and courage.

When we know which positive values are important to us, and we try to live by those values, we are more likely to make the 'right' choices in life and be happy. In contrast, when we use our negative character traits and make 'bad' choices based on 'anti-values' such as jealousy, dishonesty and selfishness, we may hurt other people as well as ourselves, and become unhappy.

It may be hard to remember to live by our values when things get tough. But that's when it's even more important and when we need the support and guidance of those around us. For example, if we accidently break something, it may be tempting to lie and blame someone else. By being dishonest, we cause pain to others and, in the end, to ourselves when we get found out and punished. By being true to our values, we can take responsibility, tell the truth and apologise. People will respect us for that and know they can trust us in the future.

Learning about positive values helps you to build a kind of a 'toolkit' in your head and your heart, so that you can make good decisions and choices in life. The more you learn and live by your core values, the more you will be able to know yourself and live a more content life.

This book is one of a series of books that focuses on character and values.

"I would like to share with you what I have found out and perhaps encourage you to live with more compassion in your life."

"Hi, my name is Sam and I'm 10 years old. I recently became very interested in learning more about values, especially the value of compassion. I feel as if I have found a way of living in a better way, helping myself and people around me to be happier.

I would like to share with you what I have found out and perhaps encourage you to live with more compassion in your life.

I live with my mum, dad and little brother Jack. Jack is different from most other little brothers. He was born blind and has grown up never having seen anything. This makes him different from anyone else I know, but in many ways, Jack is just like any other little brother – annoying, argumentative, naughty. At least that's how I used to see him.

If I'm being really honest, I used to resent all the attention that Jack got from so many people. But that was before I learned about compassion. That changed so many things for me."

"I have to tell you that I'm football crazy and so are most of my friends. My best friends are Alexis and Isla. I'll tell you more about them later."

"It all started with an event at school a few months ago.

Every year, I enjoy watching a big charity event on TV, and Mum and Dad always donate money. This year, my school announced they were going to support the charity.

I listened carefully as my headteacher, Mrs Turner, explained in assembly what the money they raised would be used for. She showed us a short film from the charity's website and we saw children of all ages having struggles and challenges in their lives.

Some of the children lived in very poor conditions and didn't have parents to look after them. Some young children actually had to look after their parents because they had become very ill. I was really surprised to learn that some children had such huge responsibilities in their lives and I found myself feeling really sorry for them.

Then the film showed some children who had special needs and weren't able to do lots of things because they didn't have support or the type of equipment they needed, and my thoughts turned to Jack. Although he is blind, I don't really think of him as having special needs. He seems to live life to the full, with everyone always helping him with everything and making a big fuss of him all the time.

But in the film, there was a boy who was blind and couldn't do anything because he had no one to help him. I had a huge feeling of sadness in my heart and I suddenly realised that both of us were very lucky to have parents who love and care for us so much, a lovely home and everything we need.

Mrs Turner suggested we raise money so that the charity could give support to the children in the films and others like them. I was very moved and wanted to help.

Later, in class, we decided to plan a fancy-dress football match and ask people to give money for watching the match. Our teacher, Mr Burne, suggested that the staff could form a team and play against the pupils.

Through the day, I kept remembering the assembly and thinking about the children in the films. After tea, I decided to do some more research about the charity. I wanted to show Mum what I had seen.

As we watched one short film after another, I started to feel terrible. The films showed more children who needed so much help. I was shocked to see children in other countries who worked in rubbish dumps, selling what they found to give money to their parents. I saw badly disabled children who desperately needed special care.

The films also showed how much the charity was able to help by providing support, equipment, care and places for children to go where there were other children like them and they could make friends. I felt very lucky for everything in my life and really wanted to help as much as I could."

"Later that night, I had an idea. I would make posters to advertise the football match so more people were aware of the children in the films."

"The next day, I printed pictures of children from the charity's website and wrote about their stories on the posters advertising the match. I worked really hard and it took me ages to make ten posters.

Mum couldn't believe it, and told me I had been really kind. But at school, Mr Burne was amazed and told me that I had shown real compassion.

I wanted to know the difference between kindness and compassion so Mr Burne explained to me that compassion is a value that makes you want to help when you see someone suffering. Kindness is also a value, but you can show kindness to someone when they aren't suffering."

"I thought about times when I had been kind, like when I helped Mum carry the shopping in from the car the other day and when I made Dad breakfast on Father's Day.

Then I thought about how I felt when I watched the films that made me want to create my posters. I felt sad, really sad. I even felt a bit angry that this could happen to children just like me. I felt that it's just not fair that some children are really poor, or have to live with people who can't care for them. If they are sick or have special needs, they should have what they need.

I felt a strong urge to help them. The charity looked to be making a big difference to their lives so I thought that if I could help to raise even more money, more children would be helped.

When I explained all of this to Mr Burne, he gave me a wonderful smile and told me that I was showing a great deal of compassion by taking this kind of action. Something inside me felt good.

I was learning so many new words and concepts. Compassion, values, character...

I asked Dad what values he lived his life by. He took a while to reflect on his values and told me they were *love*, *respect*, *justice*, *compassion* and *equality*.

I hadn't really heard Dad use these words before, but it turned out that he used these values all the time in his work. I found out that his job was helping people who have come to this country from other countries where there is war – people who are terrified for their lives and have had to leave their own homes to find safety. They are called asylum seekers or refugees.

He helps them to find somewhere safe to live and to settle in a new country. He often talks about how wrong things are in the world and how he wants to make a difference to the lives of people who are suffering. He feels very strongly that war is wrong and that everyone deserves the best chances in life, no matter where they come from.

Over the next few weeks, I learned more about values, and I noticed them all around me. When I watched people suffering, I felt very sorry for them. This is the value and feeling of *sympathy*.

If you see someone else in a situation that you have been in yourself, you know how it feels. When you can put yourself 'in someone else's shoes', you are showing the value of *empathy*.

Mum talked about *kindness,* which is strongly linked to *compassion*. Sometimes, people choose to only be kind to people they like or to their family or pets. They may like to seem as if they are kind, but when they live with the value of kindness in their heart, they show kindness to people they don't necessarily know or even like. Compassion is slightly different to kindness as the person showing compassion is taking action to help stop or lessen someone's or something's suffering."

PEACE

respect

ToLERANCE

COURAGE

GRATITUDE

generosity

"There are many other values that can be linked to compassion, such as *love, care, peace, respect, tolerance, courage, gratitude* and *generosity.*"

"Once, I was watching a programme when the values of *justice* and *compassion* were mentioned. I found this interesting and wanted to find out more, so I did some research.

I found out that a person who has a compassionate character may take action based on how much they want to help and to relieve the suffering of someone or something.

A person acting from the value of justice will act depending on how fair they think something is. How right or wrong the situation is. They judge how a person, people, animals or the environment have been treated. This bad or unfair treatment may lead to suffering – and the compassionate person will want to help stop or lessen the suffering. They may also take action based on the value of justice to try and stop the suffering at the root.

Sometimes people take action because they value justice as much as, or even more than, compassion."

"Shortly after finding out about this, I actually had an experience of seeing the importance of justice. I noticed that my friend Isla had become very quiet and seemed to be unhappy. I found out that she was being bullied."

"I felt very sorry for Isla and wanted to comfort her and ease her suffering. I felt compassionate towards her as well as lots of other feelings, which grew out of my value of *friendship*.

However, I mostly felt very angry! Isla had been treated so badly that she was too scared to tell anyone about what had been happening, and this made me angry because it wasn't fair. Bullying is wrong!

So, as well as showing compassion to Isla, I persuaded her to be courageous and come with me to tell a teacher she trusted."

"The teacher was also very compassionate and saw that Isla was being treated disrespectfully and unkindly. She agreed that this wasn't fair and immediately acted to put a stop to the bullying.

Isla was very grateful to me for helping her."

"Mum and Dad were proud of me when I told them what I had done for Isla. They said I had shown courage and compassion to help a friend who was having a hard time.

One evening I talked to them because I was having a hard time myself. I wasn't being bullied or anything like that. It was something quite different. I was finding my maths lessons very difficult. Maths was one of my favourite subjects but we were learning some really tricky things about fractions which I just didn't seem to be able to understand.

I was used to finding maths quite easy and now I was struggling to understand something that lots of other people seemed to understand. I felt bad, a bit stupid compared to everyone else. I was cross with myself for not understanding.

Mum and Dad taught me something more about compassion through this experience. They said that many people are very compassionate towards other people, but sometimes they give themselves a really hard time.

They said I should be kinder to myself and think about 'self-compassion'. This means treating yourself with the same kind of compassion, care and kindness as you would treat those you care about.

They encouraged me to think about what advice I would give to a friend who was struggling in some of their lessons. I knew I would encourage a friend by telling them that lots of things are hard and you won't always find things easy. You should do your best and ask for help when you need it.

I now realise that when times are tough and when things go wrong, we can only try our best and, by showing self-compassion, we are recognising that we are human and are going through what everyone else does. This actually makes us even more compassionate towards others as well."

"I was feeling as if I was on a 'Compassion Mission'. I wanted to see if I could spot more examples of compassion in the world, so I started to really notice what was going on around me and also look for compassion in books and on the TV.

I became so focused on this value, I was able to spot it in many places. For example, I noticed that one of my best friends, Charlie, was extremely compassionate with people who I didn't know. I watched as Charlie played with different people almost every day – and it was always people who didn't seem to have anyone else to play with. Charlie made the effort to look out for people who seemed on their own, or lonely. He actually cheered them up and looked as if this made him happy too.

Thinking about it, Charlie actually had loads of friends and was popular with everyone. One day, I decided to ask him about why he played with so many different people. Charlie told me that when he was much younger, he had to go to a new school where everyone knew each other and no one wanted to be his friend because he was new. That made him feel very lonely. He remembered that no one made the effort to get to know him for ages and he was so unhappy.

Charlie also told me something surprising, which was that he was actually very shy.

I wouldn't have imagined that, as Charlie was always with people and seemed to be having a great time.

Charlie explained to me that it takes courage to talk to someone new, but when he sees someone who looks lonely and sad, he knows how that feels and that makes him care about helping them so they don't feel the same way he did at his new school. This explains how Charlie has so many friends!

I was able to recognise some values that Charlie was using. He was showing *empathy*, *kindness*, *courage* and *compassion* to help other people – and to help himself too.

I found it was easy to spot lots of other examples of compassion too:

- Teachers in the school who would give up their lunchtime to help pupils with problems.

- The site manager, Mrs Miles, who helped the Nature Club to build a bug hotel after school.

- The wonderful support staff in the classrooms whom I had never really noticed, but now I noticed, how much they helped children they worked with – especially those with special needs.

One day I looked out of the window and saw my brother Jack in his PE lesson. He was working on throwing and catching a ball. By Jack's side was Miss Graham, who was helping Jack with care, enthusiasm and encouragement. Jack obviously found this activity extremely challenging, but Miss Graham was so caring with Jack and so determined to help him succeed in his efforts that he was laughing and trying his very best for her.

I think that many children with Jack's disability would have given up, but Miss Graham (who I later found out also had a brother who was blind) was a compassionate, empathetic friend to Jack and helped him to persevere and succeed.

Now, I also notice examples of people acting with compassion in many different ways. When I was watching my favourite nature programme last week, they were talking about climate change and the damage that was being done to the world.

This got me quite worried but as I carried on watching, I found myself captivated by a report about people who are called 'conservationists', who work hard to protect the environment and endangered animals. I could see that these people were showing compassion to the environment.

I can see in many books and films that there is a fight between good and evil, and that lots of the characters fighting for 'good' are doing so out of compassion. I love the character of Dumbledore in the *Harry Potter* books. He is an incredibly compassionate character because he fights so hard to save the world from the evil Voldemort.

When I talk to Mum and Dad about my 'Compassion Mission', they smile and tell me they are so proud of how I am noticing compassion in the world around me. I think that if everyone in the world knew about compassion and tried to act more compassionately, so many things would be better. I decided to read about how people could become more compassionate – to themselves and to others."

66**I** have discovered that by reflecting in the morning and evening on how compassionate I have been during the day, I can recognise how I am developing compassion and noticing it more around me. I found out that some people actually meditate to become more compassionate, and I would like to learn to do that, but for the moment, I feel that by just taking time to be still and quiet and to reflect on compassion is a wonderful way to deepen this value in my life.

A great example of this happened last week. One morning, before school, I was sitting quietly on my bean bag in my bedroom and just letting my mind think about being compassionate to other people.

I thought about the children on the charity's website, and then my thoughts started to focus on my grandma, who has been living alone since my grandad had died last year.

Mum often visits her because she says that Grandma is very lonely and quite unhappy now. I saw that my mum is being very compassionate towards her own mum, by trying to help her be less lonely.

While I was reflecting on this, it was as if my heart had a thought, and I realised that it would be compassionate of me to visit Grandma too. I hadn't realised that she was so lonely. I knew that she loves playing card games with me, so I thought I could teach her a new game and spend some more time with her."

"I really value this reflection time and the thoughts it brings up. I have even made myself a little Compassion Diary and I write about what I have noticed each day."

"One morning, I woke up feeling bothered by a thought: 'What stops people being compassionate?' I really feel that if there was more compassion in the world, things would be very different and there wouldn't be all the suffering we see on TV and in the news.

As I sat on my bean bag and reflected, I realised I could start to answer this tricky question.

Deep down, I had started to notice when I found it difficult to act compassionately. There was a new boy in my class called Alexis whom I didn't like very much. No one did. Alexis didn't speak very good English, and he didn't smile very much. In fact, he had a very miserable face and he didn't seem to want to be anyone's friend. At lunchtime, he sat by himself and, worst of all, he said he hated playing football.

Some of my friends had started to tease Alexis about this, calling him names as he sat by himself on the bench in the playground. I hadn't done this but when Alexis came to talk to me one day, I had ignored him and run over to play with my friends.

As I thought about how I had acted with Alexis, an uncomfortable feeling grew in my stomach. I asked myself why I had behaved like that. I came up with reasons, like Alexis seemed strange, that he wasn't like me, that it was difficult to understand what he was saying and that he didn't smile.

I must admit, I didn't feel great thinking like this. I had been honest with myself about my feelings, but something kept bothering me and later when I was reflecting on compassion, I could see Alexis in my mind's eye.

Surprisingly, new thoughts started to come to me and I found myself thinking that perhaps Alexis needed a friend and someone to show him some compassion. Maybe he felt like Charlie did when he started his new school.

I thought some more about Alexis. I wondered why he was so unhappy and where he had come from. Perhaps he was having a really tough time. Maybe he had come from another country and had to leave all his friends behind. I also realised that I was judging him badly because he didn't like football. But I'd never even wondered what he did like.

The more I thought about Alexis, the more I realised what a difficult situation he was in. I thought about what it must feel like to be in Alexis's shoes. Starting a new school in the middle of the year must be hard. I imagined I would worry that no one would want to be my friend or that they would like different things from me.

I noticed I was feeling empathy. I also tried to imagine what it was to be in that situation and not be able to speak the same language as everyone else. That must make you feel very isolated.

Alexis was on my mind so much that I talked to Mum and Dad about him. They listened hard and asked me to think about my assumptions. I was believing that because someone was different in some ways from me, that they weren't very nice, and so I didn't want to be their friend. Mum and Dad helped me to see that I didn't really know anything about Alexis. None of us did. I decided to find out more about him, and remembered what Charlie had said about needing courage to talk to someone new."

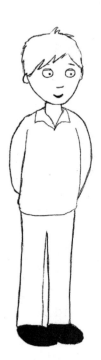

"The next day, I watched Alexis more closely and I actually started to feel some compassion for him. He looked shy and almost scared at times. I had a sudden thought and wondered if he may have been bullied in the past, or if he was maybe a refugee and had had to leave his country.

I remember feeling very nervous as I approached Alexis in the playground that day. I realised I had made judgements about him without knowing any facts and I wanted to offer him some support. Alexis smiled shyly at me and seemed pleased I had come over. It was difficult at first for me to understand Alexis because his first language wasn't English, but I was able to learn that he had indeed come from another country where there was a war and that his father was still there. He had a small brother called Nikos who was about the same age as Jack. But Nikos was very ill and in hospital after the journey to England and Alexis was worried that Nikos was going to die.

We actually became great friends in just a few days. I learned a very important lesson through this experience. I realise that it is hard to show compassion all the time, but by reflecting on your true feelings, and by appreciating other values such as sympathy, kindness, empathy and courage you can feel better about yourself and help others to feel better too.

It would have been easy to have carried on ignoring Alexis and even being mean to him. I was so glad I hadn't done that. I would have felt bad about myself. Instead, I had used my values, grown as a person and made a wonderful friend.

Sadly, Alexis's little brother, Nikos, died a few days later. I was glad that I could be there as a friend and a big support to Alexis. I also found myself being extremely grateful that my own little brother was around and, having been through this experience with Alexis, I am now much more appreciative of Jack and don't find him nearly so annoying after all."

"One day, Dad told me that he was really impressed with how I was helping others and the way I had become really interested in the concept of compassion.

Part of Dad's job was to work with organisations who supported refugees and asylum seekers. He was well known for training people and for giving talks about compassion in the workplace.

Dad knew some very interesting facts about the actual benefits to people's minds and bodies when they developed a more compassionate way of being.

He taught me that people who deliberately practise being more compassionate produce less levels of a certain hormone than other people.

The hormone 'cortisol' is sometimes called 'the stress hormone' and can have quite a damaging effect on people. By showing more compassion, people seem to feel less stressed.

Dad had noticed that being more compassionate also helps people to become happier. It helps others around you to become happier as well.

One of Dad's favourite quotes was by The Dalai Lama who said: 'If you want others to be happy, practise compassion. If you want to be happy, practise compassion.'"

"The charity football match was a huge success! The fancy-dress costumes were brilliant with lots of funny animals turning up to play, and there was even an alien from outer-space on the staff team!

I had worked with some friends, including Alexis, who was now one of my best friends, to come up with a special rule so that the teams would be more fairly balanced. Because we were about half the size of the staff, the goal net into which the staff had to score was half the size. This made it doubly tricky for them to score.

It was a great match, full of fun and determination from both sides to win. The score was equal with just a minute to go. I was extra-determined to win! I am always being told I am extremely competitive, and although I know I am a great team player, I love nothing more than to win at football.

In the last minute, I had the ball and was running as fast as I could towards the goal. A teacher who looked remarkably like Dumbledore was chasing me down, but I seemed to get some extra energy from all the children shouting my name. I kicked the ball as hard as I could, just as the teacher tackled me. But the ball was headed for the outside of the goal and I groaned.

As I lay flat-out on the ground, Isla came from nowhere and, with great skill, flicked the ball into the top of the net! The final whistle went, and the pupils cheered for what seemed like an hour. The staff team couldn't believe they had lost by a single goal. But what a brilliant game it had been and so much money had been raised for the charity.

"I was so glad I had spent time and effort on the posters. I watched people reading them and many extra donations were given on top of the price of the ticket."

I like to think that I had managed to help people think about values like sympathy, care and kindness and I hope they felt a deeper feeling of compassion in their hearts.

Mum said that I had helped people to reflect on the suffering of others and think about how grateful they were for what they had. She said the money they had donated was more generous than anyone expected, and that was a sign that they were feeling more compassionate.

This had all been a huge journey for me. I felt as if I had learned so much about myself, other people and different values – especially compassion.

I am sure I will continue to reflect every day and deepen my understanding of these concepts. I really feel as if I want to help people see that they can make a difference – and that it starts with working on ourselves before anything else."

WHAT CAN YOU DO?

Can you think of ways in which you could become more compassionate? Here are some suggestions. Think about which other values or qualities you are using at the same time. For example:

- Put your 'compassion glasses' on. Not real glasses of course, but focus on looking for examples of compassionate acts all around you. Look for role models of compassion to be inspired by and notice when people don't show compassion, and the consequences of their actions.

- Be compassionate to someone who is feeling lonely. Give them a smile and talk to them.

- You may need to use the values of courage, empathy, sympathy, confidence, respect, patience and understanding.

- Show compassion by caring for a pet. Initially, this may be fun, but sometimes it's hard to remember that without your constant care, your pet will suffer. You may need to use the values of care, responsibility, cooperation, positivity, kindness and determination.

Practise compassion.

- Try to reflect every day on how you have treated other people and how you have been treated.

- Think about how you showed positive values and compassion, and also think about how you could have acted differently – more kindly or more respectfully, for example.

- Take a few minutes each day to be still and quiet and to just reflect – or even not think about anything at all and let thoughts come to you. This is a way of practising compassion for yourself.

There are many more ways to show compassion. If you have enjoyed this book and learning about compassion with Sam, please share what you have learned with the people you know. Remember:

If you want others to be happy,
practise compassion.

If you want to be happy,
practise compassion.

(The Dalai Lama)

RECOMMENDED READING, ORGANISATIONS AND WEBSITES

BOOKS FOR CHILDREN

McCloud, C. (2013) *Have You Filled a Bucket Today? A Guide to Daily Happiness for Kids*. Nelson Publishing. This book introduces an idea that everyone has an "invisible bucket". These buckets are used to hold your good thoughts and feelings about yourself. When you do something kind, you help fill someone else's bucket.

Munson, D. (2000) *Enemy Pie*. Chronicle Books. This tells a classic story of judging a book by its cover or making judgements about people based on insignificant details. After spending quality time together, the two enemies learn that they actually get along quite well.

Silverstein, S. (2010) *The Giving Tree*. Particular Books. This book shows the continual generosity and kindness of the tree, and how much the actions of the boy affected the tree. It can be used to teach children that kindness is important, but that you should never give up so much that you suffer.

BOOKS FOR ADULTS

Brown, B. (2013) *The Gifts of Imperfect Parenting: Raising Children with Courage, Compassion and Connection*. Sounds True. Brené Brown invites us on a journey to transform the lives of parents and children alike. Drawing on her 12 years of research on vulnerability, courage, worthiness, and shame, she presents ten guideposts to creating what she describes as "wholehearted" families where each of us can continually learn and grow as we reach our full potential.

Dalai Lama (2012) *How To Be Compassionate: A Handbook for Creating Inner Peace and a Happier World*. Rider. The Dalai Lama's message in this book is as renowned as he is himself: that compassion is essential for individuals and for the world. This is very much his subject for, when we think of His Holiness, we immediately think of the compassion he embodies, and to which he has devoted his entire life.

Hawkes, N. (2013) *From My Heart: Transforming Lives Through Values*. Independent Thinking Press. This transformational book advocates a positive mental attitude that aims to empower young people with a sense of their own future and their potential to shape it according to their own purpose. It discusses the benefits of caring for yourself and others, as well as providing medical evidence to support these ideas.

Snei, E. (2014) *Sitting Still Like a Frog*. Shambhala Publications. This little book is a very appealing introduction to mindfulness meditation for children and their parents. In a simple and accessible way, it describes what mindfulness is and how mindfulness-based practices can help children.

Stafford, W. (2012) *Just a Minute: In the Heart of a Child, One Moment...Can Last Forever!* Moody Publishers. Wess Stafford, President of Compassion International, shares stories and experiences to introduce you to the difference you can actually make anywhere on the spectrum of child development.

ORGANISATIONS/CHARITIES

Children in Need:
www.bbcchildreninneed.co.uk

Charter for Compassion:
www.charterforcompassion.org

Values-based Education:
www.valuesbasededucation.com